P9-CDF-658

A0002601526219

STICK INSECTS

Geoff Miller

Grolier
an imprint of
SCHOLASTIC
www.scholastic.com/librarypublishing

WITHDRAWN
KIRTLAND PUBLIC LIBRARY

Published 2009 by Grolier
An Imprint of Scholastic Library Publishing
Old Sherman Turnpike
Danbury, Connecticut 06816

© 2009 Grolier

All rights reserved. Except for use in a review, no part of this book may be reproduced, stored in a retrieval system, or transmitted in any form, or by any means, electronic or mechanical, including photocopying, recording, or otherwise, without prior permission of Grolier.

For The Brown Reference Group
Project Editor: Jolyon Goddard
Picture Researchers: Clare Newman, Sophie Mortimer
Designer: Sarah Williams
Managing Editor: Tim Harris

Volume ISBN-13: 978-0-7172-8074-2
Volume ISBN-10: 0-7172-8074-8

Library of Congress Cataloging-in-Publication Data

Nature's children. Set 6.
p. cm.
Includes index.
ISBN-13: 978-0-7172-8085-8
ISBN-10: 0-7172-8085-3
1. Animals--Encyclopedias, Juvenile. I. Grolier (Firm)
QL49.N387 2009
590.3--dc22
2008014675

Printed and bound in China

PICTURE CREDITS

Front Cover: **Corbis**: Michael and Patricia Fogden.

Back Cover: **Shutterstock**: Kurt_G, Ra'id Khalil, Dmitrijs Mihejevs, Dr. Morley Read.

Corbis: Ron Austing 13, Anthony Bannister 18, B. Borell Casals 30, Michael and Patricia Fogden 9, Chris Hellier 40–41, Wolfgang Kaehler 34, Joe McDonald 22, Buddy Mays 10, 33, Geoff Moon 6, Robert Pickett 17; **Fotolia**: Geza Farkas 29; **NHPA**: G. I. Bernard 21, 25, Stephen Dalton 14, 37, Pavel German 45, Stephen Krasemann 26; Photos.com 2–3, 42; **Shutterstock**: Humphrey Grimmet 46, Eric Isselée 4, Dr. Morley Read 5.

Contents

Fact File: Stick Insects 4
Insects Everywhere 7
Habitat 8
Big Insects 11
Sticks and Leaves 12
In Sections 15
The Exoskeleton 16
Breathing 19
Camouflage 20
Plant Eaters 23
Wings 24
Flying Sticks 27
Sharp Senses 28
Slow Movers 31
Reproduction 32
Laying Eggs 35
Many Eggs 36
Nymphs 38

Growing Up 39

Feature Photo 40–41

Limbs that Regrow 43

Pet Sticks 44

Defenses 47

Under Threat 48

Words to Know 49

Find Out More 51

Index 52

FACT FILE: Stick Insects

Class	Insects (Insecta)
Order	Stick and leaf insects (Phasmida)
Family	Stick insect family (Phasmatidae)
Genera	There are many genera of stick insects
Species	At least 3,000 species
World distribution	Almost worldwide; more common in tropical and subtropical regions
Habitat	Any area where plants are plentiful, especially tropical rain forests
Distinctive physical characteristics	Sticklike body; spindly legs; green, gray, or brown in color; some types grow to 12 inches (30 cm) long
Habits	Conceal themselves among leaves and stems; active mainly at night; remain motionless for long periods; lay hundreds of seedlike eggs
Diet	Stick insects feed exclusively on plants

Introduction

Stick insects are among the most unusual-looking insects. They resemble twigs or leaves. Some even have spines like the thorns of certain plants. Stick insects are amazing for many different reasons. Many types of stick insects can produce young without the help of a **mate**. Young stick insects can regrow lost legs! Stick insects are also popular and easy-to-keep pets. Unfortunately, in the wild, many types of stick insects are under threat as their natural **habitats** are lost to human development.

Stick insects are also known as walking sticks or stick bugs.

With its twiglike body, the stick insect can cleverly disguise itself as part of a plant.

Insects Everywhere

Almost everywhere in the world, there are insects. Flies, butterflies, beetles, bees, wasps, ants, and dragonflies are just a few of the many kinds of insects. There are more than 1 million different types, or **species**, of insects, and new ones are discovered by scientists every year.

Insects have been around for hundreds of millions of years. Over time, they have changed, or **adapted**, themselves so that they can survive in many different habitats. Stick insects, as their name suggests, actually look like twigs or small branches. With their slender, twiglike body, they can safely hide in bushes and trees. Over millions of years, these insects have adapted themselves to suit their conditions. They now look like the plants on which they live.

Habitat

Stick insects thrive in tropical **rain forests**. The tropics are the parts of the world nearest the **equator**. There, it is hot and sunny all year round. Stick insects are particularly abundant in the rain forests of Africa, Asia, and South America. In these forests, there are plenty of fresh plants for the stick insects to eat. However, tropical forests are not the only places where stick insects live—you can also find them in North America, Australia, and the warmer parts of Europe around the Mediterranean Sea.

This stick insect lives in the Amazon rain forest in South America.

This giant stick insect is 1 foot (30 cm) long. If it sat on your arm, it would stretch from your fingertips to beyond your elbow.

Big Insects

Insects are the most successful of all creatures. Almost two-thirds of Earth's animals are insects. There are at least 2,000 species of stick insects. To help sort out the different types of insects, scientists place them into large groups called **orders**. Stick insects belong to the group known as Phasmida (FAZ-MID-UH), which comes from a Greek word meaning "having a strange appearance." This name refers to stick insects' ability to look like the branches on which they live.

Insects come in a great range of sizes. Some are almost too small to see, while others grow to 14 inches (35 cm) long. Stick insects are among the biggest insects. Adult stick insects usually measure from 3 to 6 inches (8 to 15 cm) long, but the largest can be 12 inches (30 cm) long!

Sticks and Leaves

The stick insect family includes stick insects and their close relatives, the leaf insects. Stick insects get their name from their spindly body. They stay for many hours in the same spot without moving, blending perfectly with the plants on which they live. Leaf insects are just as remarkable. They do an excellent impression of a leaf. It can be an amazing sight to see what you thought was just another leaf suddenly begin to walk. They are so well disguised that other insects, even other leaf insects, sometimes take a bite out of them by mistake! Leaf insects are found in most of the places where stick insects live, particularly in tropical rain forests.

This Japanese leaf insect imitates both the color and shape of a leaf.

By carefully placing its legs so they blend naturally with the twig, a stick insect makes its disguise even more effective.

In Sections

Although there is a huge variety of insects, they all have the same basic body structure. The word *insect* means "in sections," which accurately describes the way an insect's body is formed. If you look very carefully at an insect, you will notice that its body is made up of three separate parts: the head, the **thorax**, or middle section, and the **abdomen**, or rear.

Stick insects have a long, slim body so that they can hide themselves among the trees and branches. Not all types of stick insects have wings, but those that do have slender, delicate wings. These are kept folded back along their body to maintain their sticklike disguise. The longest part of a stick insect's body is its abdomen, which is divided into smaller parts, or segments. The segments are joined by flexible joints that allow the stick insect to bend its body.

The Exoskeleton

Inside a human body, there is a framework of bones called a skeleton. Around the skeleton are muscles and skin. Insects do not have a bony skeleton on the inside like humans. Instead, they have a strong outer casing that surrounds their body like a suit of armor. An insect's outer skeleton, or **exoskeleton**, is made up of many sections of tough material fitted together with flexible joints to allow for movement.

Every so often during its life, a stick insect needs to **molt**, or shed, its exoskeleton so that it can grow. The insect grows a new exoskeleton underneath the old one. Then the old casing cracks open, letting the newly covered insect emerge. The new outer casing is soft at first, and the insect must be careful to avoid danger until the casing hardens.

Up close, a spiny stick insect has a frightening face!

Holding onto the bottom of a leaf, a stick insect creeps out of its old outer casing.

Breathing

The cast-off casing of a stick insect very often has fine threads hanging from its inside. These strange threads actually help insects breathe.

Like all animals, insects must breathe in oxygen from the air to live. But unlike humans, insects do not have lungs. An insect takes air into its body through a number of tiny openings called **spiracles**. A stick insect has ten pairs of these holes along its body—two on its thorax and the rest along its abdomen. The holes connect to a network of fine tubes that carry the oxygen to where it is needed in the insect's body. The fine, shiny threads left hanging from the stick insect's discarded outer casing are actually the remains of its old set of breathing tubes!

KIRTLAND PUBLIC LIBRARY

Camouflage

When soldiers go into battle, they often disguise themselves to fool their enemies or to make themselves difficult to see. The patchy colors on their uniforms and vehicles, called **camouflage**, help them blend in with their surroundings. Animals also use disguise to hide from **predators**. With their twig-shaped body, stick insects are masters of disguise and can be almost impossible to pick out from the surrounding plants. Colored green, gray, or reddish brown, they are very difficult to spot among leaves and branches. A stick insect can remain almost motionless for hours at a time, looking exactly like a plant's stem. Sometimes when a breeze blows, it will sway gently backward and forward to complete its masterful disguise.

Can you spot the stick insect hiding on this moss-covered branch?

This stick insect, from Argentina in South America, is nibbling on a blade of grass.

Plant Eaters

Stick insects spend most of their time living among trees and bushes. Their favorite foods are the leaves and stems of plants. Unlike many insects, which catch and eat other creatures for food, stick insects are pure **herbivores**—they eat only plants. They feed mostly during the night and particularly enjoy fresh, green leaves and tender shoots. Stick insects use their powerful jaws, called **mandibles**, to munch their food. Some species eat only one type of plant. Others are not so picky and will eat many different types of plants.

Stick insects have a big appetite. Sometimes they gather in large groups called **swarms**. A single swarm has been known to strip trees completely bare of their leaves.

KIRTLAND PUBLIC LIBRARY

Wings

The wings of insects are as varied as the insects themselves—think of the beautiful wings of a butterfly or the long, delicate wings of a dragonfly. Not all insects are able to fly, but those that can have either one or two pairs of wings. Some do not have any at all, such as most types of ants. Stick insects are unusual because some species have wings, while others do not.

Most insect wings are thin and light and are almost see-through, or transparent. A network of tubes, called **veins**, running down the wings makes them rigid and strong. Insects such as flies and wasps have only a few veins running down their wings. Other insects, such as dragonflies, have intricate patterns that crisscross their wings. Experts can tell a lot about different insects by studying the patterns on their wings.

A stick insect flutters its strong but light wings.

A stick insect opens its wings as a warning to frighten predators away.

Flying Sticks

Stick insects that can fly have two pairs of wings. The front wings are usually not very large. The rear pair is more important for flying. The wings are joined to the stick insect's body at its thorax. When the wings are not in use, a stick insect keeps them tucked away alongside its body. In this position, the front edges of the wings look a little like dying, or withering, leaves. The underside of some stick insects' wings are brightly colored. If the insect is attacked, the wings can be quickly unfolded to reveal a bright flash of color that may scare the predator away.

Stick insects are not very good fliers. Sometimes instead of using its wings to fly, a stick insect may use them like miniature parachutes. If it is disturbed by a predator, the insect falls from its branch, unfolds its wings, and glides safely to the ground.

Sharp Senses

To discover what is going on around them, stick insects have eyes and **antennas**. Insect eyes are not the same as human eyes. Like many insects, stick insects have **compound eyes**, which are made up of thousands of tiny **lenses**. Compound eyes enable insects to see movement in all directions at the same time—almost as if they have eyes in the back of their head. Each tiny lens adds to the overall picture that the stick insect sees. Some types of stick insects have several other eyes, too. These "simple" eyes are not as advanced as their compound eyes. They pick up only basic information such as color and brightness.

As well as having excellent eyes, a stick insect has antennas that look like two little **aerials** at the front of its head. Tiny hairs covering the antennas pick up chemical signals in the air and also help the insect keep its balance.

Notice the large compound eye and the two long antennas on this stick insect's head.

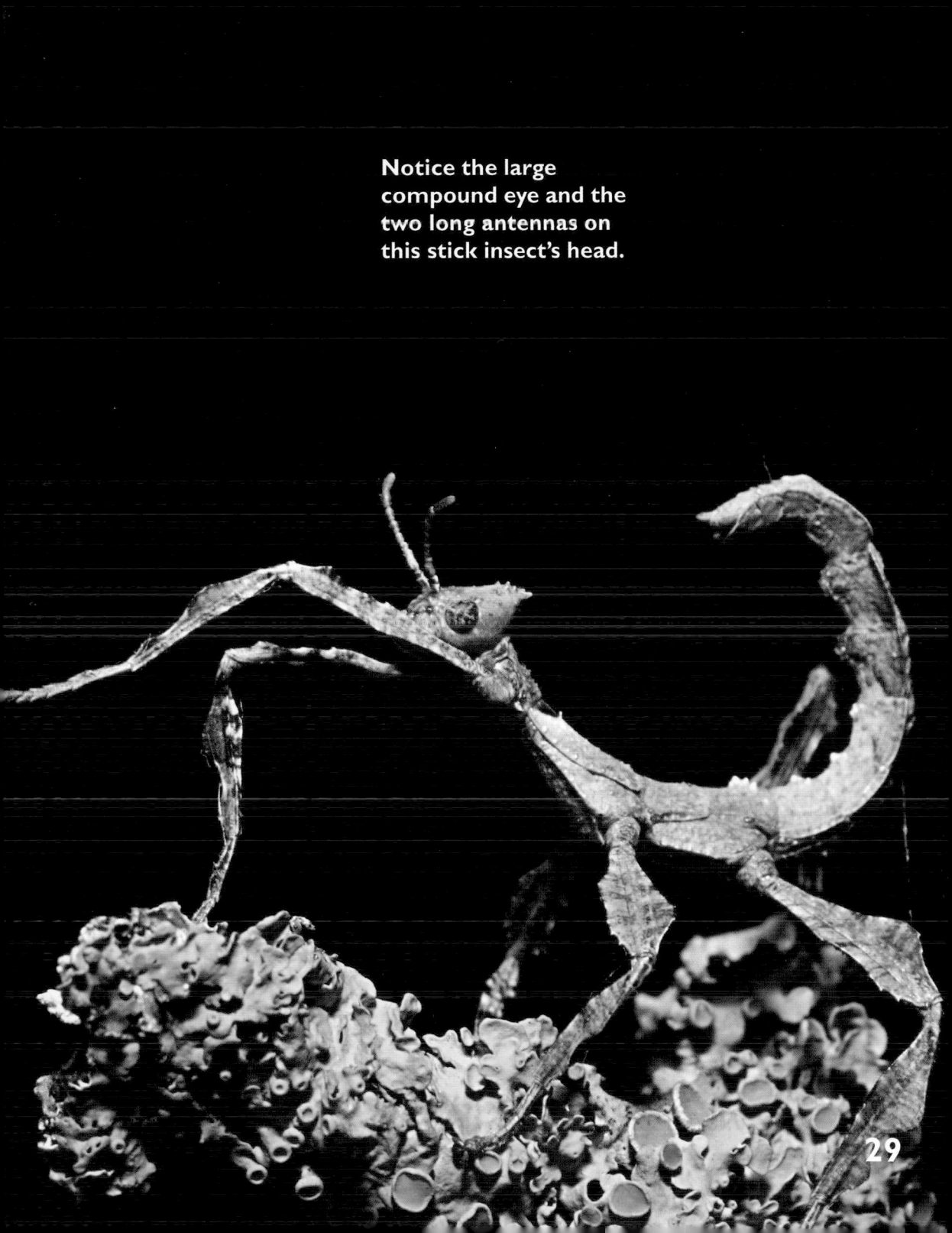

Safely hidden from predators, a stick insect hangs onto a tree with its sticky pads and tiny claws.

Slow Movers

Unlike grasshoppers and crickets, most stick insects cannot jump or leap. They are slow-moving creatures. That helps explain why they need to camouflage themselves so well. If they were easily seen, they would soon be attacked and eaten by faster-moving predators.

A stick insect moves its three pairs of legs slowly and carefully along the leaves and branches. Once a good resting place has been found, it often hangs in what looks like a dangerous position—jutting out stiffly into the air. Stick insects can hold on and stay in these difficult positions because they have little claws and special sticky pads on their feet. Some stick insects that live near streams can cling tightly to rocks while fast-flowing water washes over them.

Reproduction

Stick insects are unusual because, depending on the species, they reproduce in two different ways. In some species, all of the insects are females. A special process allows their eggs to develop without being fertilized by a male stick insect. In other species, there are both male and female stick insects. When it is old enough to breed, the male goes in search of a suitable female partner.

A much smaller male stick insect sits on top of the female to fertilize her eggs.

A female stick insect searches for a safe crack in the bark of a tree where she can lay her eggs.

Laying Eggs

About two weeks after mating, the female stick insect is ready to lay her eggs. She lays them through a special tube at the tip of her abdomen called an **ovipositor** (O-VUH-POH-ZUH-TUR). Many types of stick insects simply drop their eggs onto the ground. But the females of some species are more careful and deliberate. Others bury their eggs or hide them among the cracks in the bark of a tree. Some even attach their eggs to leaves or branches with a special glucy substance that oozes from their body.

Some species have a more spectacular method of laying eggs—they flick, or catapult, them over a wide area. The female suspends herself upside down from a branch and arches her abdomen before straightening up to throw the eggs to the ground some distance away.

Many Eggs

Stick insects lay a large number of eggs, often as many as 200. The eggs come in a variety of shapes and sizes, depending on the species. The smallest eggs are about the same size as the head of a pin, while the largest are less than half an inch (1 cm) long—roughly the size of a fingernail.

All stick insect eggs have a very tough outer shell for protection. They look a little like seeds or tiny nuts. Some eggs are shiny and smooth, while others are textured with patterns. At one end of the egg, there is a tiny cap, or lid, from which the baby, or **nymph**, stick insect will eventually emerge. A tiny hole at the other end lets moisture and air into the egg. That allows the nymph to breathe and develop inside.

A nymph stick insect will hatch through the lid of each of these nutlike eggs.

Nymphs

It can take a long time for stick insect eggs to hatch out—from four to eight months. Throughout this time, the nymph stick insect is growing and developing inside the egg.

When a baby bird hatches, it smashes open its eggshell. When a stick insect hatches, it simply pushes off the egg's special lid and climbs out through the opening. It breaks free of the egg by pulling itself out headfirst and hauling the rest of its body after it. Inside its egg, a nymph stick insect lies tightly coiled up like a spring, but upon emerging it stretches out its body and may be as much as eight times as long as its eggshell!

Growing Up

Young stick insects are born into the world as almost a perfect copy of their parents. Over the next three to six months, the nymph sheds, or molts, its exoskeleton several times. Every time it molts, the insect almost doubles in size. The body of some stick insects is covered with sharp spines to deter predators. These spines, too, grow larger each time the nymph molts.

In those stick insect species that have wings, the wings first appear as little buds on the sides of the nymph's body. Only when all the stages have been completed are the wings fully formed.

An insect's exoskeleton is made of a tough substance called chitin (KY-TIN).

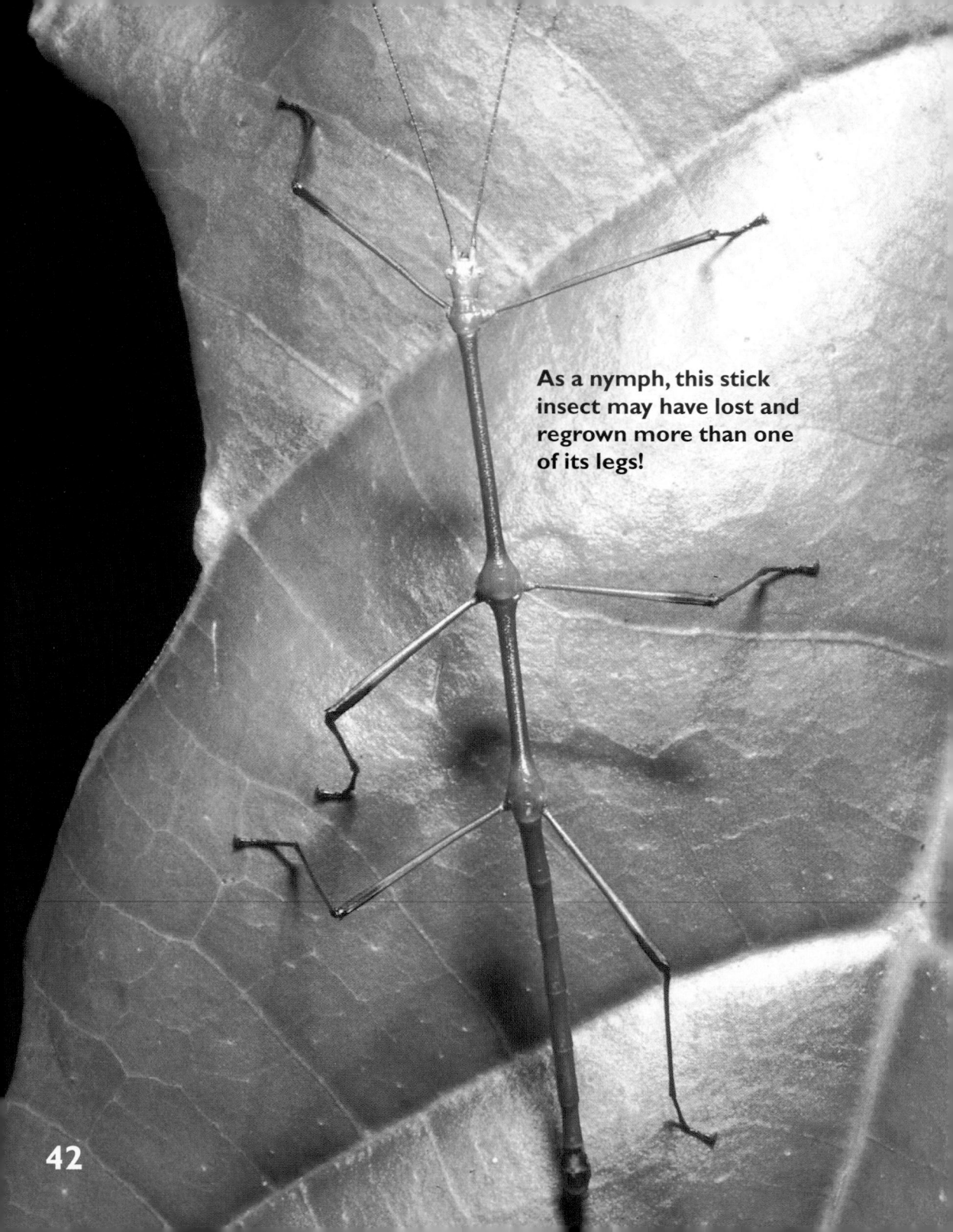

As a nymph, this stick insect may have lost and regrown more than one of its legs!

Limbs that Regrow

Young stick insects develop wings and spines. They can also **regenerate**, or regrow, a lost leg when molting. If attacked by a predator, the stick insect can give up a leg in order to escape. Each time the insect molts, the lost limb will gradually grow back. After three or four molts, a new limb will have grown to replace the one that was lost. The new limb never quite grows to full size and will always be slightly shorter than the original. If the insect loses one of its antennas, that, too, can be replaced. Instead of growing another antenna, however, another leg appears in its place! When stick insects reach adult size, they no longer molt, so only nymphs can replace body parts in this way.

Pet Sticks

Many types of stick insects make good pets. These species include the Indian stick insect, the Vietnamese bark, and the pink-winged stick insect. As pets, stick insects are easy to care for. They should be kept in a large cage with fine mesh walls. Such a cage is known as a **vivarium**. Stick insects survive well at room temperature, which is about 22°C (72°F). The insects should be given fresh leaves to eat. Their favorite leaves include bramble, privet, lettuce, and hawthorn.

Pet stick insects are fun to watch, especially when they molt. It is best not to handle them too often because they are delicate and easily damaged. Species that can fly will need to exercise their wings once a week—for example in a sealed room with no other pets, especially cats, around.

Stick insects are easy to breed. Some species, such as the Indian stick insect, are only female, so one pet can soon produce many young eggs that will hatch into young insects. Pet stick insects can live for up to one year.

Pet Australian stick insects may bite with their jaws or pinch with their spiny legs if handled too much.

This stick insect might drop to the ground, pretending to be a real stick, if attacked by a predator.

Defenses

A stick insect's main defense against possible predators is its camouflage. But stick insects also defend themselves in other ways. They often try to surprise an attacker with a display of sudden, unexpected behavior. One way they do that is to curl their long tail over their back like a scorpion. Another way is to suddenly show a bright flash of color from under their wings. Some stick insects will quickly twist and tumble, dropping to the ground. There, they lie motionless, pretending to be dead. They will often remain like this for hours, until they are certain that the hunter has moved away.

If all else fails, some stick insects can produce a foul-smelling liquid. Some spray the liquid at enemies, scaring or even blinding them. Others cover themselves with the liquid, making their body smell unpleasant.

Under Threat

While stick insects are very good at avoiding their natural enemies, some human activities pose a serious threat to these masters of disguise. In many areas, farmers spray chemicals called **insecticides** onto their crops to protect them from harmful insects. These chemicals can remain in the environment for years and kill many innocent insects, including stick insects.

The biggest threat to stick insects, however, is the destruction of their habitats. All over the world, woodlands and rain forests are being cut down to make space for human development. As the trees and bushes disappear, so do the stick insects. The habitats of stick insects need to be protected for these remarkable insects to survive.

Words to Know

Abdomen	The rear part of an insect's body. The abdomen contains the stomach and the parts females use to lay eggs.
Adapted	When an animal gradually becomes better suited to its habitat.
Aerials	Metal rods or wires used for sending out or receiving radio waves.
Antennas	Feelers on top of an insect's head that are used for smelling, touching, and tasting.
Camouflage	Patterns or colors that help an animal blend into its surroundings.
Compound eyes	Large eyes found on many insects. Each is made up of many lenses.
Equator	An imaginary circle around Earth, midway between the North and South poles.
Exoskeleton	The hard outer covering, or casing, of an insect's body.
Habitats	Types of places where animals and plants live.
Herbivores	Animals that eat only plants.
Insecticides	Chemicals designed to kill insects.

Lenses	Parts of the eye that focus light.
Mandibles	The sharp cutting parts of an insect's mouth.
Mate	Either of a breeding pair; to come together to produce young.
Molt	To shed an old exoskeleton.
Nymph	A young stick insect.
Orders	In animal classification, groups of families of animals.
Ovipositor	A female insect's egg-laying tube.
Predators	Animals that hunt other animals.
Rain forests	Dense tropical forests in areas of high rainfall.
Regenerate	To regrow a lost body part.
Species	The scientific word for animals of the same kind that breed together.
Spiracles	Tiny holes in an insect's body casing for taking in air.
Swarms	Huge gatherings of insects.
Thorax	The middle part of an insect's body.
Veins	Thin, hollow tubes that support an insect's wings.
Vivarium	A home for a pet stick insect.

Find Out More

Books

Kelly, D. A. *Stick Insects*. Bugs. Farmington Hills, Michigan: KidHaven Press, 2004.

Markle, S. *Stick Insects: Masters of Defense*. Insect World. Minneapolis, Minnesota: Lerner Publications, 2007.

Web sites

Indian Walkingstick or Laboratory Stick Insect
www.enchantedlearning.com/subjects/insects/orthoptera/Indianwalkingstick.shtml
Facts and a diagram of a stick insect to color in.

Stick Insect
animals.nationalgeographic.com/animals/bugs/stick-insect.html
A profile of the twiggy bugs.

Index

A, B

abdomen 15, 19, 35
antennas 29, 43
Australian stick insect 45
balance 28
body 6, 7, 15
breathing 19, 36

C

camouflage 12, 13, 14, 15, 20, 21, 30, 31, 47
casing *see* exoskeleton
chitin 41
claws 30, 31
compound eyes 28, 29

E, F

eggs 32, 34, 35, 36, 37, 38, 44
exoskeleton 16, 18, 19, 39, 41
eyes 28, 29
feeding 8, 22, 23, 44
feet 31
flying 24, 27, 44

G, H, I

growth 16
habitats 5, 7, 8, 48
hatching 38
Indian stick insect 44
insecticides 48
insects 7

J, L

Japanese leaf insect 13
jaws 23, 45
leaf insects 12, 13
legs 14, 31, 42, 43, 45
lenses 28
life span 44

M, N, O

mating 32, 33, 35
molting 16, 18, 39, 43, 44
nymphs 36, 38, 39, 43
ovipositor 35

P, R

pads 30, 31
pets 5, 44, 45
pink-winged stick insect 44
predators 26, 27, 31, 39, 43, 46, 47
regeneration 5, 42, 43

S, T

simple eyes 28
spines 5, 39, 43, 45
spiny stick insect 17
spiracles 19
swarms 23
tail 47
thorax 15, 19, 27

V, W, Y

veins 24
Vietnamese bark 44
vivariums 44
walking 12
wings 15, 24, 25, 26, 27, 39, 43, 44, 47
young 36, 37, 38, 43, 44